FEAR NOT

By
ARMAN STEPHENS

FEAR NOT

Copyright 2003 by Arman Stephens
ALL RIGHTS RESERVED

All Scripture references are from the Authorized King James Version of the Bible, unless otherwise noted.

To order this book and others written by
Arman Stephens and Dee Stephens,
or to
Order Tapes please write to

Faith to Live By Ministries
P.O. Box 970
Bethany, Oklahoma 73008

ISBN 0 –9716610-7-3

FTLB Publications
Published in the United States of America

But now thus saith the Lord that created thee, O Jacob, and He that formed thee, O Israel, Fear not: for I have redeemed thee, I have called thee by thy name; thou art mine. When thou passest through the waters, I will be with thee; and through the rivers, they shall not overflow thee: when thou walkest through the fire, thou shalt not be burned; neither shall the flame kindle upon thee. For I am the Lord thy God.

Isaiah 43:1-4

TABLE OF CONTENTS

For I have redeemed you	13
I have called you by your name	37
I will be with you	61
When you pass through the Waters	89
I am the Lord your God	113

INTRODUCTON

"You Devil. I'm going to Kill you Preacher Man just as soon as I get my gun. I'm going to do it in front of everybody so they can all see. This Holy Ghost devil is coming out."

That was the message written on a flattened piece of Styrofoam cup and slid under the front door of the Church. As I read it my mind immediately went to the Word of God.

Psalm 27:1-3 **"The Lord is my light and my salvation; <u>whom shall I fear</u>? The Lord is the strength of my life; <u>of whom shall I be afraid</u>? When the wicked came against me to eat up my flesh, my enemies and foes, they stumbled and fell. Though an army may encamp against me, <u>My heart shall not fear</u>; though war may rise against me in this will I be confident."**

There came a peace over me, that I knew had to come from God. I began to rejoice in the fact that God had promised to protect me and all my house, which I concluded also meant all the families of the Church as well.

Psalm 91: 1-3 says, **"He who dwells in the secret place of the Most High shall abide under the shadow of the Almighty.** "I will say of the Lord, <u>He is my refuge and my fortress; my God, in Him will I trust.</u>" Surely He shall deliver you....

As I continued to meditate on God's Word, I was confident that no harm would come, and I moved into that place of rest talked about in the Book of Hebrews chapter six.

It makes no difference what the circumstances, you can find calm and peace as you put your trust in Christ Jesus. I trust as you read, that faith, and rest will be yours.

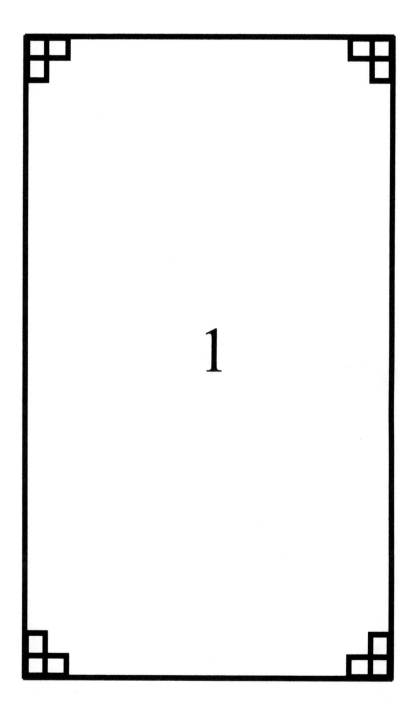

1

CHAPTER ONE

I HAVE REDEEMED YOU

Thus saith the Lord "that created thee". One could not exhaust the subject of God's creative ability. But you know the story in the book of Genesis where God stepped out onto nothingness and out of nothing He spoke words, and things came into existence. Nine times in the first chapter of the book of Genesis, "God said . . ." And when God spoke, something happened. God said, **"Let there be light."** There was light. God said **"Let there be land."** There was land. God said **"Let there be a Heaven and an earth."** There was a Heaven and an earth. God said **"Let there be fish of the sea and fowls of the air."** Every time God said, He created something. He had confidence in His word and in His ability. When God spoke, things happened. When God spoke, things that did not exist became something. His words have power to create, because when He spoke, things that were not became things that are. There was no earth prior to His speaking it into existence. There were no fish of the sea, or birds of the air, or animals of the field. There was no sun or moon; but when God said, **"Let there be . . ."** Then it was.

And God said to Israel, **"thus saith the Lord that created thee, O Jacob, and he that formed thee, O Israel . . ."** Reason in your mind what is being said. Listen to what the Lord the creator of all things is speaking. **"now thus saith the Lord that created thee . . . FEAR NOT."** <u>Don't be Afraid</u>. The one who made you in His likeness and in His image, the God who made everything and that by whom all things exist and consist said, **"Don't be afraid."** Get this imbedded in your mind firmly God the creator of all things said "FEAR **NOT.**"

If someone were to walk up to you and tell you, "Don't be afraid", it would only mean something to you in relationship to the ability of that individual to keep you from being afraid. If that individual had the physical strength and size and ability to give you confidence that he could take care of any situation that would arise, you would have no reason to be afraid. If you were walking down a dark alley in which you thought there would be someone waiting for you to attack you, but you had a friend with you that was 6'8", and weighed about 295 pounds without an ounce of fat on him very strong and trained in hand to hand combat, and he says, "Don't be Afraid, I'm here to

Take care of you,"... It means something, doesn't it? But you walk through that same dark alley with a little, Mr. Milk toast type of individual who weights 89 pounds they kick sand in his face every time he goes to the beach, with no power or strength at all, and he says, "Don't be afraid"... You're not going to have much confidence in his words, are you?

But since God, who created all things, and has all power, who made everything by the spoken Word of His mouth, by whom all things consist and are held together, said **"Fear Not.,"** then do not be afraid.

What is fear? According the Bible concordances, fear is <u>that which is caused by intimidation of an adversary.</u> Therefore the Lord is saying, Don't' let your adversary intimidate you, because I have created you and I am the Lord thy God.

Who is your adversary? The Bible

says that the devil is your adversary, and he goes about as a roaring lion seeking whom he may devour. He is just running around looking for somebody who doesn't know that they are not supposed to be afraid. Someone who will allow fear to come into their life. The devil will jump and pounce upon them and try to make them think that he has conquered them. But the Lord says **"Don't let you adversary intimidate you."**

The devil is not a gentleman, and he doesn't walk up to the door of your house every day, ring your doorbell and say. "Hi, I'm your friendly adversary. I'm going to tempt you today." He may ring the front doorbell, then run around to the back door while you go to the front door. Then he will sneak in and get you from behind. He will not do things legal or honest. There is no truth in him; he does nothing but lie, and try to steal from you, hurt you, destroy you and

If possible, kill you. That is the devil's whole purpose. John 10:10 says, **"The thief comes not but to steal, kill, and destroy."**

Many times, when I was growing up, my Grandmother would ask me to go out to a little shed behind her house where she had all her home canned goods and her deep freeze, and ask me to bring something from there. Oh, it was dark and spooky to me being only 7 or 8 years old. I would go out and get what she sent me for, and when I would start back to the house, it seemed like a mile back, although it was only about 50 to 75 feet. And every step that I took, it seemed as though there was something breathing down my back.. The faster I ran, the faster it seemed to run. By the time I got to the door, I was huffing and puffing and couldn't even open the door for the fear that had gripped me. There was no cause for fear, because there was nothing to be afraid of. I was being intimidated by the darkness.

That's like the devil, he roars at you like a lion, trying to make you fear. He tries to intimidate you with a loud roar. When in fact he is only imitating a lion. If we really understand our relationship with God, and I hope that by the time you finish this book you will, you will realize that the devil has been stripped of all his power, and there is no reason for you to fear.

When our daughter was about 2 or 3 years of age she would say, "this is a lion," and she would very timidly and quietly say, "roar, roar, roar." That is about the way the devil is. He has been stripped of power, he has no more strength, God made a show of him openly, removing his authority over you.

In the Bible the phrase "Fear Not" Is mentioned 74 times in the Old Testament. And in the New Testament Jesus said 16 times, "Fear Not, neither be Afraid". Ninety times altogether, God said, **"Fear Not, neither be Afraid."**

Yet we allow things around us every day (the pressures of life), to come in and intimidate us and cause us to fear. But if we are in Christ Jesus and we know Him as the Lord and the Savior of our life, there is no reason that we should ever allow the devil to intimidate us and cause us to be frightened or alarmed! God said again and again, "Fear Not"… "For I have redeemed thee"…

Vine's expository dictionary says, "Redeem (from the Greek word Exagorazo) means, "to buy"; it denotes to by out completely; especially of purchasing a slave with a view to his freedom; to buy for one's self."

The Lord who created you said, "don't let your adversary intimidate you and make you frightened of afraid, or alarmed,

Because I have bought you for Myself that I might set you free..." The Apostle Paul said in his letter to the Corinthians, "Do you not know that your body is the temple of the Holy Spirit who is in you, whom you have from God. And you are not your own? For you were bought at a price; therefore glorify God in you body and in your spirit, which are God's." 1 Corinthians 6:19-20.

When Jesus died on the cross of Calvary, He gave His life. He bought you, the slave of Satan, and brought you out, that you could be free and He brought you into the righteousness of God, Translated out of the kingdom of darkness and into the Kingdom of Light, so you would no longer be walking in the darkness and the blindness of sin.

Under the Old Testament Law, God said to the people of Israel, "don't ever sell your land. The Land is Mine. But, if you get into a financial bind, and you don't have any other option, then you are permitted to sell your land; and the person who buys it can give you money for it. And as things get better, and you want to do so, you can buy the land back and the person that bought it from you must sell it back to you. If it gets to the point where you don't have the money and you can't buy it back, you may have a very close relative, your next of kin, come as a kinsman redeemer, buy back the land that you sold, that it may be your possession again.

We sold out to sin; to the devil. Everything we had — our life, our possessions, our spirits, all the dominion, power and authority that God gave to man, when He created Adam and put him in the Garden of Eden and said, "Dress it, prepare it, take good care of it... This is the land that I have given to you". Adam sold the possession that God had given him and said was his for ever. He committed treason; he transferred title and deed of that which belonged to God over to the devil.

Approximately two thousand years ago, Jesus Christ, the Son of Almighty God, the Redeemer of mankind, went right down to Satan, where our life had been sold out and said, "I'm going to buy back every thing you have that belongs to them. That was Eternal Life. God created man and sold out to Satan, he sold everlasting life to Satan. Jesus came to buy back our everlasting life.

When God created man, the Bible says that God created everything perfect. If God created everything perfect, then He did not create the bodies to be sick and diseased. But when man sold out to Satan, man sold his freedom from sickness and disease. God intended for man to be prosperous. There was not one thing that Adam wanted or lacked. Everything he wanted and needed in in life was there at his disposal; but when he sold out to Satan, he sold that freedom of prosperity. Everything we had was sold out to Satan. When Jesus, our Kinsman Redeemer came, with His own blood He purchased our everlasting life, our freedom from sickness and disease, our financial prosperity, our ability to do all things and have all things that pertain to life and Godliness — Jesus, my older Brother, bought it back for me. He was my Kinsman Redeemer. "FEAR NOT. I have bought back everything that was sold. From this moment on you are totally set free from the bondage and the authority of the adversary, the devil."

Exodus 14:13 says, **"Fear not, stand still and see the salvation of the Lord."**

Exodus 20:20 says, **"Fear not, God has come to prove Himself to you."**

Psalms 118:6 says, **"I will not Fear what flesh can do to me."**

Isaiah 8:12 says, **"Neither fear ye their fear."** There are a lot of people who are afraid of everybody else's fear. He said don't fear their fear! **"fear thou not I am with thee."** To that we say, Glory to God!

Then we come over into the New Testament and read;

Galatians 3:13 says, **"Christ has redeemed us from the curse of the law, being made a curse for us, that we might be the righteousness of God in Christ Jesus."**

He has redeemed us! What from? From the curse of the law. What is the curse of the law? Read Deuteronomy 28 verse 16 through the end of the chapter, and you will find out what the curse of the law is. But Jesus has redeemed us! He bought us back, away from the curse of the law.

In Galatians 4:5 it says, **"redeemed them that are under the law."** In Galatians 4:5 it says**, "redeemed them that are under the law."**

Titus 2:14 says, **"that He might redeem us from all iniquity and purify us unto Himself a peculiar people, zealous of good works."**

I Peter 1:18 says, **"He has not redeemed us with corruptible things, but with His precious blood."**

Revelation 6:9 says, **"Thou has redeemed us by your blood."**

This is a marvelous truth from the Word of God. Listen to what it says, one more time as I give it to you in a more literal translation. "But now thus said the Lord (the Lord is Yahweh, which means the God who created all things, and by Him everything exist, and remains) Fear Not, don't be intimidated by your adversary, who causes alarm and fear. For I have bought you back with the price of my precious blood, in order that I might set you free. I bought you for myself so that you may be free." Now that is what the Lord God said. If you have fear in your life, there is no reason for it to be there. If you are the redeemed of the Lord, one who has been bought from sin and Satan by the precious blood of Jesus Christ, then fear has no place in your life.

Romans 8:15 tells us that, **"God has not given us the spirit of bondage again unto fear, but you have received the Spirit of Adoption whereby we cry Abba Father."** You see God is my Father, Jesus is my elder Brother, and He is the one who had the right to go and buy me back, and He did. Now He says, Fear not, for God has not given us a spirit of fear.

I John 4:18 says, **"There is no fear in**

Love; but perfect Love cast out all fear."** What is perfect Love? Jesus, God is perfect Love. Where does God live? If you have accepted Jesus as your savior, then He lives in you. You are the dwelling place of God.

II Corinthians 4:7 says, **"But we have this treasure in earthen vessels."** What treasure is he talking about? The very life flow of God; the very nature of God living inside of us. Therefore, if He is in me and He is Love, then I am love and perfect love casts out all fear. I will not fear, because I know that God has bought me, and redeemed me, and made me His own and set me free.

The devil and all of his cohorts can take you under if you are on God's side and you have been set free from sin. Let me say something and make it very clear. The devil cannot cross the bloodline of Jesus Christ. If you have been redeemed by the blood of

Jesus, the devil cannot cross the blood. The devil will never be able to posses your spirit, as long as the blood of Jesus Christ covers your life. You have been set free. There is no reason for you to fear. Fear is a thing of the past to those who know who they are in Christ Jesus. When you know you have been redeemed and bought back then fear goes. It does not exist any longer in our lives. Fear should never enter into the life of a born-again child of God.

Now that does not mean you will never be tempted to fear. The devil will tempt you to fear; but when that thought comes to your mind, you tell the devil that he is a liar and I will not accept what he is trying to put in my mind. Say , "I take authority over it because perfect love casts out all fear."

Many people fear about the world situation, they fear about their jobs, they fear about their home, they fear about their family, and many other things. I've had some to say to me, "Pastor, I'm afraid and I just worry about this all the time." And I say, "There is no reason for you to worry. The Lord said to cast all your worries and anxieties on Him because He is concerned about you and it matters to Him about you. So don't worry about it." They said back to me, "But if I don't worry, who will?"

You don't need to worry or be afraid because God has delivered you from worry. He has redeemed you from sickness. He has delivered you from fear. He has redeemed you from anxiety, and emotional turmoil. God has redeemed you from all the problems that come from the curse of sin, and the curse of the law. It's time we start living that redeemed life. Therefore, the redeemed of the Lord shall return to Zion and with a shout they shall praise the Lord because God has given to us the redemptive power and the glory of God!

Hallelujah! We have been redeemed from the curse of the law. God has given us victory. If you don't know what I'm talking about and fear is in your life because of the world situation and all the problems that are happening. If you have fear because of a Doctors report. If you have fear because of your financial position. Or fear concerning any other thing. Let me tell you that you can have relief from that fear today through Jesus Christ. By accepting Him as the Lord and Savior of your life. I have been writing this to encourage Christians as to what God has done for them. But I want you to know that if you are not a Christian, you can have a part in God's redemptive plan. Jesus Christ cam come into your life and redeem you from all of the fear and all the frustrations and all the problems of life.

God has given us victory.

Therefore, the redeemed of the Lord shall return to Zion. They shall return. What is that talking about? The redeemed of the Lord, those who have been bought back, are going back to the place God intended for them to be in the first place. They are intended to live for the Glory of God and to shout victory and praises to God.

Isaiah 51:11 says, **"Therefore the redeemed of the Lord shall and come with singing unto Zion; and everlasting joy shall be upon their head: They shall obtain gladness an joy; and sorrow and mourning shall flee away."**

The redeemed of the Lord, those that have been bought back, those that belong to the Father God through Jesus Christ our Kinsman Redeemer, who bought us with His precious blood, said we shall return to Zion, to the place of everlasting blessings with joy in our hearts, mourning and sorrow all flee away. Why? Because we have been bought with a price, the blood of Jesus Christ, God's dear Son , our older Brother. Therefore we will not FEAR. We will walk in the freedom that God intends for us to. We need to say, **NO FEAR HERE,** because I have been redeemed.

2

CHAPTER TWO

I HAVE CALLED BY THY NAME

"I have called thee by thy name, thou art mine." <u>CALLED</u>. The first four verses of Exodus Chapter 3 tells the story of a man who was out on the dessert side of Midian, watching after the sheep of his father-in-law. Coming around a particular area, he saw a bush that was on fire; and this bush, though it was burning, it was not being consumed. As he turned aside to see what was going on, the Lord saw that he turned aside to see, and God called unto him out of the midst of the bush and said, "Moses, Moses." And Moses said "Here am I." God had called him by Name.

Isaiah the Prophet, said that the Lord that created us, said, **"Fear not, for I have**

Redeemed you, I have <u>called</u> you by your name."

I think it is quite interesting to know that God knows everyone of us by name. I know a lot of people, and I know many of them by name; but there are many more whom I know, whose names I do not know. I can't go very many places without finding somebody I know. But I can't always remember the names of those people that I am supposed to know. Have you ever been in that position? But the Lord knows everyone of us by our name.

When God spoke to Moses and called him to do the great work that he was to do, God did not say, "Hey man, hey you, come here, I want to talk to you." No, God looked right at him out of that burning bush and said, "Moses, Moses…" And Moses heard the call of God.

In the book of Exodus, the 33rd

Chapter, Moses was talking to the lord about how He had delivered the people of Israel and the various things that had been done. And now God was angry at the people of Israel because of their committing of sin by making a golden calf and worshipping it instead of God. God was going to do something about it and Moses said to the Lord, **"See you say unto me, bring up this people: and Thou hast not let me know whom Thou wilt send with me."** The 17th verse says, **"Yet thou hast said, "I know thee by name and thou hast also found grace in My sight. And I know thee by name."** Do you know what is indicates when a person knows someone by name? It means that they have fellowship, and a relationship with that individual. There is a friendship; there is a kindredship of some sort; there is some way in which they are brought together, and there is some sort of communication between the two people if they know each other by name. In one way or another they have been introduced and they have talked to one another.

And the Lord said, **"I have called thee by thy name."** Moses said to God, **"Lord, You even said You called us by our name. You know our very name."** In the book of Samuel is a story which tells of a lady who prayed for a son because she had none. She cried and prayed before God, and God answered her prayer and sent her a son. She named him Samuel. She took him to the temple and there he dwelt with Eli as a servant in the temple. One night, the boy Samuel was lying in bed asleep. Suddenly, a voice spoke, **"Samuel, Samuel"** He ran to Eli to see what was going on and asked, "Did you call me?" Eli said "No I didn't call you, go back and go to sleep." Pretty soon Samuel heard the same voice again:

"Samuel, Samuel." The next time it happened, Eli said "Go back, and if He calls you again, you will know it must be the Lord who is calling you. Just say, Here am I, Lord. What do you want me to do?" You see God knew Samuel by name and called him by name. And, when we were called into the everlasting grace of Jesus Christ, He didn't just say, "Hey you, come here." He called us by our name and drew us to Him.

God know our name. We can't hide from God. We can't run from Him. We can't change our name and think He doesn't know who we are! God know who we are and He calls us by our name. When Jesus called the disciples, He called them by name. As Saul of Tarsus was on the road to Damascus, a light shined out of Heaven and blinded him; he fell to the ground and cried out, "Lord, who are you?" And Jesus said, **"Saul, Saul, why persecutes thou me."**

Jesus knew his name and He called him by name. He know you personally; He knows you intimately.

Now my last name is Stephens. That means when you call me Stephens that I am the son of another Stephens, because I go by the name of my father. I also have a first and a middle name, and God knows all three of them. But my last name denotes who my family is, and when you call me Stephens, that denotes that I come from the family line of Stephens. When you call me Arman, that indicates a personal relationship. But this is interesting. God said first of all, **"I have called you by your name."** Then in verse 7, God says, **"I have called you by my name." <u>GLORY TO GOD!</u>** That means that I am a member of the Family of God, and though I have a name that's given to me, I also have a name that has been given to me by birthright. I have become a child of the

Almighty God and I am in His family. He is my God, my Father and my Lord and Savior! **GLORY TO GOD!**

God said, "I have redeemed thee, I have called thee by thy name; thou art mine."—— "I have called you by your name and you are mine." Isaiah 42 :6 says, "I the Lord have called thee in righteousness…" I have called you righteous… I have called the by your name —— righteous." If we are children of God, that means we are in right standing — we have righteousness. Therefore, we are called **"righteous."**

Isaiah 45:3, "And I will give thee the treasures of darkness, and hidden riches of secret places, that thou mayest know that I, the Lord, which call thee by thy name am the God of Israel." Again He talks about calling us by name. Look over in the 63rd chapter of Isaiah, verse 15: "Look down from Heaven the habitation of Thy Holiness and of thy Glory: Where is Thy zeal and Thy strength, the sounding of Thy bowels and of Thy mercies toward me? Are they restrained? Doubtless Thou art our Father." Now who is He talking about? Who does the prophet say is our Father? God is our Father. "<u>Doubtless thou art our Father,...</u>" The prophet said that there is no doubt that God is our Father, and that we are the lineage of Abraham. And he said, "though Abraham be ignorant of us, and Israel acknowledge us not: thou, O Lord, art our Father, our Redeemer; Thy name is from everlasting." Now look at this: "God looked down from Heaven." What was the question the prophet asked Him? "What about your mercies toward me? Are they restrained?" The answer to that question is an obvious **"NO"** His mercy is not held back. And he said, "you are my Father; even though Abraham doesn't know who I am." You see I have never met Abraham, he doesn't know that I am one of his sons. And though Abraham does not know that fact, yet God is my Father; and that makes me of the same family; puts me under the same covenant with the same rights, the same privileges, the same blessings. —— They are all mine just as they were Abraham's. He doesn't know that I am his son, but I am; because God is my Father, my Redeemer (and the literal translation of redeemer is that I have been bought back). I belong to God and God's name is from everlasting.

Isaiah 63:19, speaking of Israel says, "We are Thine;" and then, speaking of the Gentiles, says "Thou never barest rule over them, they were not called by Thy name." Who is not called by God's name? All those who have not accepted Jesus as Savior. They are not called by the name of God. They don't know what it is to be called by the name of God But the prophet said, "We are called by Thy name." Get hold of this friends. Grasp this concept, because it does do something inside of us when we begin to understand that by accepting Jesus as the Lord and Savior of our lives we enter into a covenant relationship with God. God knows us by name, and He has also made us a member of the Family of God through Jesus Christ our Lord. Therefore, we have the same name that God has.

    The world is watching the born-again, Spirit-filled Christian to see how he lives; what he does, and what he does not do. We as believers, called by our name and by God's name, are of the Family of God. If our lives are out of line and out of harmony with the character of God, the world gets a false understanding of God. We need to be very sure that we are a true representative of the righteousness of God everywhere we go, and in everything we do and say. Not only has God called us by our name, He has called us by His name. Isaiah 43:1 says, **"Fear not: for I have redeemed thee, I have called thee by thy name; thou art mine."** But He doesn't stop there: verse 7 says, **"even everyone that is called by My Name; for I have created him for My Glory, I have formed him; yea , I have made him."** Understand that not only has God called us by our name; He has also called us by His name.

People are going to Judge God by us, because we are of the same family. The only God that most people in this world know is us. For He said, **"As I am , in this world so are you."** The way we live and the way we act and the way we react demonstrates our God to the world. That is why it is so important to live a good example, and not let **FEAR** rule in our lives.

In Ezekiel 16:8, *"Now when I passed by thee, and looked upon thee, behold, thy time was the time of love; and I spread my skirt over thee, and covered thy nakedness: Yea, I swear unto thee and entered into a covenant with thee, saith the Lord God, and thou becamest Mine."* God said I saw you and I loved you and I took you for my own You became Mine. He is talking about a love and his bride. What happens when a person gets married? The bride takes the name of the groom. They become one. They are no longer what they used to be. They are now one together. And when we come into Jesus, we are no longer what we used to be. We take His Name. We become like Him. We are now of Him. He knows us by our name and calls us and says, you are mine. When I married my wife Dee, she no longer was a Teague. She is a Stephens, and will be a Stephens until the day she dies.

She is now Dee Stephens. It's now legal, it's on her Drivers license, it's on her Social Security papers. Every legal document that she signs is signed Dee Stephens. I know her by name and she is mine, and I am hers! God says, "I have called you by your name and you are mine." Why are we His? Because He has redeemed us. He bought us with His Blood. He made us His, and He says that He covered us and took us to be his.

Hosea 11:1 says, *"When Israel was a child, then I loved him, and called my son out of Egypt."* This reference let's us know we are a part of the family of God. We are His. Deuteronomy 14:2 says, *"For thou art an holy people unto the Lord thy God, and the Lord hath chosen thee to be a peculiar people unto Himself, above all the nations that are upon the earth."* He has chosen, He has called us to be a peculiar people. That does not mean a bunch of freaks that go around all the time with long sad faces and never smile. Peculiar in this context means a person that is set apart for the glory of God and the service of the Lord; different than anybody else. In John 1:12 we read, *"But as many as received Him, to them gave He power to become the sons of God, even to them that believe on His Name."* His Name is involved again , isn't it? God said He has called us by our name and then He said He has called us by His Name. As many as received Him, to them gave He power to become the sons of God, even to them that believe on His Name. His Name brings you into the family of God.

In Romans 8:15, *"For ye have not received the spirit of bondage again to fear; but ye have received the Spirit of adoption, whereby we cry, Abba, Father."* (Or loving, kind, gentle Daddy.) You see, we've been brought into the family of God.

2 Corinthians 6:18, *"And I will be a Father unto you, and ye shall be my sons and daughters, Saith the Lord Almighty."*

Galatians 4:5, *"To redeem them that were under the law, that we might receive*

The adoption of sons." Who did that? Jesus did that! He e redeemed us so that we could be adopted as sons into the family of God; and because we are sons, God has sent forth the Spirit of His Son into our hearts crying, Abba, Father. **Glory to God!**

Many scriptures verify that we are known by God, and chosen by Him to be members of His family. Ephesians 1:5, **"*Having predestinated us unto the adoption of children by Jesus Christ to himself, according to the good pleasure of His will,..."*** He has chosen us to be adopted into the family of God.

Thus said the Lord that created you, Fear Not. Don't be intimidated by your adversary. For I have purchased you and bought back from Satan, (your adversary) all that was sold out, that I might be able to call you by your name and make you Mine.

Revelation 2:13 says, *"I know thy works, and where thou dwellest, even where Satan's seat is: and thou holdest fast my name,..."* Verse 17 of the same chapter says, *"...To him that overcometh will I give to eat of the hidden manna, and I will give him a white stone, and in the*

stone, and in the stone a new name written, ..." We used to sing a song a few years ago, "There's a new name written down in Glory, and it's mine, oh yes it's mine. And the white-robed angels sing the story that a sinner has come home. There's a new name written down in Gory, and it's mine, oh yes it's mine." In another passage in the Book of Revelation, it says that He gives you a name that no one else knows. I'm becoming more and more convinced of the fact that we might not be called by our name given to us at our natural birth, but the one given to us when we were born again. God has a new name written down that no man knows. He said "I have called you to be a member of <u>My Family</u>."

"Fear not: for I have redeemed you, I have called you by your name and you are mine." The thing that excites me the most and makes me the happiest is to know that we are His, and that my name is written down. Though on this earth we may have name given to us our earthly family, yet our new name is Christian, — Christ like. You see we are a member of the family of God. We have the same name God has. Do you know that's why the devils tremble and fear when we begin to invoke the name of Jesus into a situation. You say. "But Jesus is not here. He is up in Heaven sitting at the right hand of the Father." But we have the same name Jesus has; and He said <u>anytime</u> you ask <u>anything</u> in my name I will do it; the Father will give it to you. **Anything.** Not just a few things. **Anything.**

What does it mean to be a member of God's family? In Romans 8:15 it says, *"For ye have not received the spirit of bondage again to fear; but we have received the Spirit of adoption, whereby we cry <u>Abba Father</u>."* God has made us heirs with Christ , joint-heirs with Jesus. Heirs of God — that means everything God has is going be handed down to His Son. And it says joint-heirs. Under the Old Testament law, the eldest son received the greatest portion. The other received smaller amounts. But God changed the system, and He said, "I make you joint-heirs with Him." All of the inheritance of Heaven is co-equal with Jesus Christ. We are together, as far as the benefits of God are concerned.

I'm only saying, this is who God says we are; we are who God says we are, a Son of God, filled with the power of the Glory of God, with rights and privileges just like Jesus had! God changed the system. We are joint-heirs. Didn't Jesus Himself say before He went back to Heaven, "Everything I've done, you will do. The works that I did, you will do ." How come we are not doing them? You see we have His ability.

Receive the same benefits. He has called us by His name. We are a new person in Christ Jesus; old things passed away, all things become new. When we accept Jesus Christ as our personal Savior, we are created brand new just like Adam was in th Garden of Eden. Our spirit man is just made all over brand new. That is the new birth we talk about. He causes us to be born into the family of God, therefore, we now take the same name of God and we have access to the benefits of the will of God and all things that are His are ours.

"Fear not: for I have redeemed thee, I have called thee by thy name; thou art mine." **GLORY TO GOD!** I wouldn't want to belong to anybody else. I want to belong to Him. If we do know Jesus as Lord and Savior, then let's start acting like a member of the Family of God. You say, "Well, what does that mean? It simply this: Jesus said, as a family member, "I don't do any thing that I haven't seen by Father do. I don't say anything that I don't hear my Father say first." In other words everything that the Father intends to do, Jesus did it and told us to be just exactly like Him.

When you were a child did you ever play like you were somebody else, trying to be just like them? Many still, after they are grown, are trying to be somebody else. Did not God say that we were to be imitators of Him? Didn't He say to act just like He acts? Do like He does? Care just the way He cares? Love the way He loves? Do every thing that He has done? Heal the sick. Raise the dead. Cast out devils. Walk on serpents. God said to just obey Him and do everything that He does. Now, God is going through this world doing good all the time, and He will do it through us if we will allow

Him. We are the same family. And the things He did you do. Let's start being like Him. We are called by His name. We are heirs of the Father; we are join-heirs with the Son Jesus; we are children of the Kingdom of God; we are a family, we are one. You are my brother and my sister, and we are one in Jesus Christ the Lord.

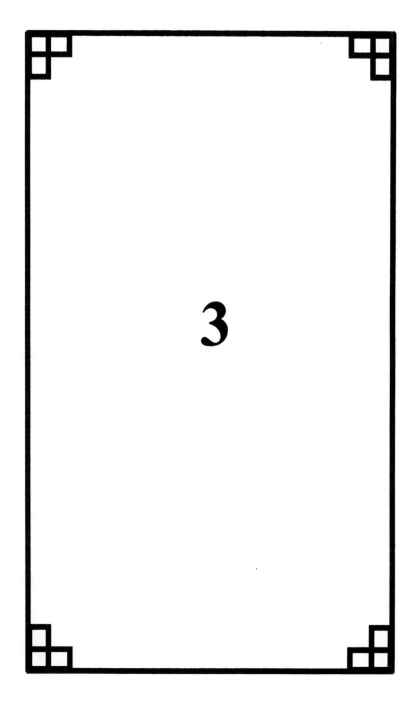

CHAPTER THREE

I WILL BE WITH THEE

Isaiah 43:1, literally translated reads, "Thus saith the Lord that created thee, O Jacob and formed thee, O Israel, (the word "Lord" is "Yahweh" which means "I AM. There is none other. I have created all things. I am the God who creates things and causes things to happen."). The one who created all things and literally causes everything to happen and hold together, has created you, O Jacob, and formed you, O Israel. Fear not. Don't let your adversary intimidate you and cause you to be alarmed or frightened; because I have redeemed you, I have bought you with a price, for Myself, with the purpose of setting you free that you might do work in this earth that I've called you to do; because I have called you by your name, and you are Mine.

He said, "Fear not, because I have redeemed you; I have called you by your name; you are Mine. When thou passest through the waters, I will be with thee, and through the, rivers, they shall not overflow thee." "When thou passest through the waters. . ." Now, in looking up the word "waters" to see exactly what the Lord was talking about, I discovered that He was not talking about an 8-ounce glass. The word "waters" that is written in this passage talks about a great amount of water, like the waters of a flood, for example. When thou walkest through the flood waters. . . Now we all know what a flood is. We realize that a flood is a little bit more than just a river, or a trickle or a stream, don't we? I have never been in a flood but I've watched on television as newscasts have given reports of floods in various stages. There is awesome power in great amounts of rushing flooding water. Imagine that powerful flood of water. "When thou walkest through the flood. . ." Now how can anybody walk through a flood? I've never seen anyone yet do it. Every time they've shown pictures of floods, if there's anybody out in it, they're going pretty fast and they're not walking, they're floating. Right. There is no walking through floods.

But the Holy Spirit said, through the prophet Isaiah, "When thou walkest through the waters (or when you pass through the floods), I will be with you. And through the rivers, they shall not overflow thee." Now when you pass through those floodwaters and through the rivers, it will not overflow, as it is used here, means "it will not inundate you". That simply means it will not drag you under or thoroughly wash you away. So the Lord said, "Don't allow your adversary to intimidate you and cause you to be alarmed or frightened, because I have bought you for Myself that I might set you free; and when you pass through the floods, I will be with you; and through the rivers, they will not inundate or drag you under or cause you to be thoroughly washed away." Why did He say that? Why is it that we can pass through the floods and through the rivers and not be inundated and washed away and dragged under? Because He is with us.

There is a clear distinction which shall be made at this point. Jesus did not say we would never go through a flood, nor did He say we would never walk through rivers of affliction. But He did say that when we pass through the floods and when you walk

In Mark 4, Jesus told the story of the sower going out to sow the Word. He said the seed is the Word of God. He talked about birds coming along and devouring it and various things happening to the seed that was sown. Jesus basically said this: those things come to destroy the Word. When the Word of God begins to come into your life, friend, you can rest assured that the devil is going to come against you like a flood. The devil will try his best to sweep you under and thoroughly wash you out. At one time I didn't really know that truth, but many years of experience have shown me clearly that Satan will try to "wipe out" the believers. The Lord said very clearly that floods will come; rivers will be there; you will face them for the Word's sake. As a matter of fact, the Word tells us that we will be persecuted for righteousness' sake. When we begin to live the righteous life, we begin to recognize that we are the righteousness of God in Christ Jesus: we are what God says we are, the righteousness of God. He became sin, that I might become the righteousness of God in Christ Jesus. Then He said that we are to do the works of righteousness.

What are the works of righteousness? Doing the things Jesus did: healing the sick; raising the dead; casting out devils; walking by faith; living an overcoming, victorious life; telling the devil where to get off and what to do, instead of allowing him to drag us down and tell us what to do and where to go; doing the works of righteousness. And Jesus said that we will be persecuted for righteousness sake.

Now, another statement made by the Lord is, *"Blessed are you when men shall persecute you and say all manner of evil against you"* There will be those who will persecute you with unfair, unloving words and attitudes when your life is manifesting the righteousness of God. People don't talk about you if you're in the same hole they're in. But you start living the prosperous, overcoming, victorious life that God says you can live and they're going to talk about you, because you're blessed. Jesus said you are blessed when people talk about you like that. Floods will come. They will be there to persecute; and it's for the sake of the Word and for the sake of righteousness. The devil doesn't persecute you for any other reason except for the sake of righteousness and the Word of God that is implanted within your heart. The devil really doesn't care about you one way or he other. The devil hates God so much that he tries to destroy God's crowning creation – **Man** – and that's why the devil is trying his best to destroy you. Not because he hates you or likes you so much. It's not because he wants you on his side because you're such a lovable person and he just likes to be around you. The devil could care less about you. The devil hates God, and he will do anything he can to destroy God. The devil things that if he can destroy Man, God's greatest creation, he can destroy God. So the devil doesn't persecute you for the sake of just persecuting you. Any flood of the devil's persecution or affliction comes on the basis of righteousness and the Word of God that's within our lives.

Now understand this one thing. Affliction does not mean sickness. The Lord said, "Many are the afflictions of the people of God." And that's where most everybody stops – right there. But read the rest of that. Many are the afflictions of the people of God, **but the Lord delivers him out of them all**. When thou passest through

I will be with you. When you go through the river, it will not overflow you. There are many examples of people who were persecuted for the sake of righteousness. Daniel is a classical example of this. Daniel prayed daily – three times a day – and it made the other people angry. So they decided, "We'll take care of him. We'll pass a law that you can't pray." Now, that happened because of Daniel's righteousness. What did Daniel do? He prayed. He sought God; they found him doing it and said, "Okay, we'll throw you in the lion's den." Now, it would look like the waters had overflowed him at that point. It would look like from any natural standpoint that the river had pulled him under and he was thoroughly washed away. **But in the midst of the Lion's den, God was with him**. God had said that He would be with him. And it seemed like when he was persecuted for His righteousness sake, that he was about to go under, but he did not go under. God sent an angel who locked the jaws of those lions. And Daniel had a better sleep than the king did in his palace.

The Bible says that the king paced the floor all night long, wondering what was going to happen to Daniel. You know, there must have been a spark of faith in him, because he came down the next morning and cried into the lion's den, "O Daniel, Daniel." Why else would a man come down and say, "Daniel, Daniel, are you still there?" I believe that if we will walk in the way of righteousness, regardless of what floods come against us; people will see Jesus Christ and the power and ability of Almighty God that brings deliverance in lives and they'll say, "Hey, I want what you've got."

Paul walked in affliction constantly. The floods and the rivers will come. They will come. Some of you are going through them right now. Some of you have been almost flooded over by the enemy. He has come against you with fear and other afflictions. **But the Lord said that we would not be overcome by them. We will not be overflowed by them.** Remember this: God said, "Thou art mine. . and I will be with you." Now when the floods come, remember this word. Paul said, under the anointing of the Holy Spirit, ***"God will not allow us to be tempted above that which we are able to bear; but with the temptation He will make a way of escape."*** There is always a way out. Don't ever lose hope or give up. Paul, standing on board a ship that had been under a storm for 14 days and nights; after they had cast off all weight of all the cargo that they had and the ship was about to go under – everything that was in that ship and said, to the captain, "Sir, fear not. Because the angel of the Lord, Whom I serve, hath stood by me this night; and he has said that everything is going to be all right."

God has clearly said unto us (God, Who created us and formed us), "Don't allow your adversary to intimidate you, cause you to be alarmed or frightened; because I have bought you with that precious blood of Mine, that I might set you free. Therefore, when you walk through the waters, and when you go through the rivers, I will be with you, and they will not inundate you or drag you down or thoroughly wash you away. "With every problem, God will make a way out. With every situation that comes against you, God makes a way out. In Isaiah 59:19 the Word says, **"When the enemy shall come in like a flood, the Spirit of the Lord shall lift up a standard against him."** When the who are we talking about? The enemy is the devil. When he comes in how? Like a flood! Overwhelming you. When he comes in with all of the cares and the problems of life; when he comes in with a lack of finances; when he comes in with a lack of physical ability; when he comes in with all these things and tries to make you think that he's going to pull you under; the Lord. . .the Lord will. . .the Spirit of the Lord will raise up a standard against the devil and push him back from you. You will not have to fight in your own strength. The Lord Himself will fight for you. Let me give you an example. When the Children of Israel were at the Red Sea, the army of the Egyptians was behind them, mountains were on one side, desert on the other, and a flood of swollen water was in front of them. What did they do? "When thou passest through the waters, I will be with you. The waters rolled back they passed right through them. At the Jordan River, the same thing happened to them. The waters just parted and they walked right through. God was with them! When it seemed there was no way; when it seemed they were flooded under; when it seemed they were being thoroughly wiped out; God came to the rescue! And whenever the waters of affliction come upon you, whenever it seems that you are being flooded, Jesus is there to bring you through. When the enemy comes at us with the flood of physical sickness, the Lord has said, **"I will be with you."** ". . .the Spirit of the Lord will lift up a standard against him." Our part is to continually confess the Word of God and to believe God's promises for our physical health. (Isaiah 53:5, James 5:14-16). If healing does not appear to come quickly, and we still have the physical symptoms, our tendency is to wonder, "How long must I keep this up?" The answer is that we must keep it up until we get the desired results.

I believe that it is God's will that we walk in divine health and divine prosperity, and that all of the things God has said are ours, are ours. **We are what God says we are. We are healthy. We are prosperous. We are kind. We are loving. We are gentle. We are what God says we are.** Kenneth Copeland has pointed out that the problem with most of us is, we say we're a sick person trying to get well. We believe we are a poor person trying to become rich. We act like a sad person trying to be joyful. The Word of God says, "We are healed." It's the devil who is trying to make us sick. We are prosperous, and it's the devil who's trying to make us poor. We are joyful and it's the devil that's trying to make us sad. We need to get our thinking right and we will find the Lord going through the problem with us. I am not a sick man trying to get well. I'm a healthy person that the devil's trying to make sick. I am healthy! Why? Because Jesus is healthy. I am in Him and He is in me. If we are one and the same, then we are healthy. Jesus is healthy; I am healthy; we're health. The enemy will come in and try to make us think, "Oh, I've got the sniffles this morning. I'd better do something; I'm getting sick." And we'll listen to that voice before we'll take the Word of God again and again. But the Lord said, "When the enemy comes in like a flood, the Spirit of the Lord will lift up a standard against him."

In Matthew 7:24 Jesus says, *"Therefore whosoever heareth these sayings of mine, and doeth them, I will liken Him unto a wise man, which built his House and the rain descended, and the floods came, and the winds blew, and beat upon that house; and it fell not: for it was founded upon a rock."* Jesus didn't say the floods would not come. Jesus did not say the rain would never be there. But He said, "The man that hears My Word and then does **MY WORD.....THAT IS THE KEY.** Remember that every promise of God is based on a condition and God said it's not enough just to hear what He has to tell us; we have to be a doer of the Word as well as a hearer of the Word. Until we start doing what we hear the Lord says, we'll never have anything we desire of the Lord. But Jesus said, "He that hears my statements and does them is like the man that has built his house upon the rock; and when the rains come and the floods beat against it, it will stand." **"If God be for us, who shall stand against us."**

Romans 8:38 & 39 says, *"For I am*

persuaded, that neither death, nor life, nor angels, nor principalities, nor powers, nor things present, nor things to come, Nor height, nor depth, nor any other creature, shall be able to separate us from the love of God, which is in Christ Jesus our Lord."

When the enemy comes in like a flood; and we pass through the waters and through the rivers, the Lord will be with us and it will not overflow us, drag us under or wipe us out. "Thus saith God, the Creator of all things, Who made you and formed you; Don't let your adversary intimidate you or cause you to be alarmed or frightened, because I have bought you with My precious blood for the purpose of setting you free. I have called you by your name; and you are Mine. When you pass through the floods, I will be with you. When you walk through the rivers, they will not overflow or inundate or drag you under and wash you thoroughly away." Psalm 77:19 says, "Thy way is in the sea, and Thy path in the great waters, and Thy footsteps are not known." A way is made, a path through the waters, that you walk upon. Habakkuk 3:15 says, "Thou didst walk through the sea with thine horses, through the heap of great waters." "You walked through the waters." That reminds me of the three preachers that were out fishing one time. One of the fellows decided that he would get something to eat. They were on a boat away from the shore, and he just stepped out and started walking across the water. The next man decided he would do the same thing. He got out and walked across the water. The next man stepped out, but he began to sink, and he cried out, "Why can't I walk on the water like the rest of you?" They said, "Well, you have to know where the rocks are." And that is true for us also, we must know where our solid footing is.

What is the rock? Jesus said, "I make a path. I make a way through the waters." Then He said that I am to walk on that path and that water. When the disciples were out on the Sea of Galilee one night, suddenly Peter and the others looked up and saw a ghost and were frightened. Jesus said, "Don't be alarmed; it's just Me." What was Jesus doing? He was walking on the water. Peter said, "Lord, if you can do it, I want to do it, too." Jesus said, "Come." Peter got out and walked on the water. Jesus walked on the water; and we can walk on the waters of affliction, through the power of Jesus Christ in us; because **He said, *"I will never leave thee nor forsake thee. I'll go with you even unto ends of the earth*** (see Matthew 28:20). When faced with the water of affliction pouring in, don't give up believing in God. Don't give up trusting in the Word of the Lord; because the Word of God will never fail. *It's easier for Heaven and earth to just completely disappear than it is for the Word of God to fail.* God's Word will never fail (see Matthew 24:35).

One time I was standing on the Word of God about a particular promise; and I laid the Bible on the floor and I stood right on it and said, "Now God, I am not figuratively standing on the Word, but I'm literally standing on the Word of God. You know something's got to be done. If I fail at this point, that means Your Word has failed." You know what? His Word did not fail. It never has failed and it never will. God has said to you, dear friend, going through the floods of affliction from the enemy the devil, "Don't be afraid; because when you pass through those waters, I'm with you." I want to ask you a question; you answer in your own mind. First of all, how many of you believe that Jesus is the Son of Almighty God? Now, how many of you believe that He has the ability to meet the need and the crisis of every person's life? How many of you are going through a crisis that seems as though it's about to overflow you? How man of you believe that if Jesus were to come in person and stand now in front of you and ask you what you would like for Him to do, and you asked Him to do it, believe He would do it for you?

Let me tell you a little secret. We can't have any more assurance that what the Word of God has given in Isaiah 43; "When you go through the flood, I will be with you; and through the rivers, it will not overflow or drag you under, or cause you to be washed away." If we are who we say we are in Christ Jesus, there is nothing that can drag us under or wipe us out; because Jesus has promised it. The New Testament tells us that we have a new promise and a better covenant than Abraham had, with more sure promises and benefits; because Jesus gave His blood to make sure that they come to pass.

Regardless of what we're going through; it's not more that we can bear. Neither is it something that no one else has ever gone through; because the Word says there has no temptation take us, but such as is common unto man. I'm not minimizing the problems that we have. I'm not trying to say there is no problem and that we're just making a mountain out of a molehill. We may have a great problem, but we don't need to have that problem any longer; because the very God who created us and formed us has promised, **"If you ask any thing in My name, I will do it."** The very God Who created us and formed us has promised that "all things are ours that pertain to life (everything on this earth) and godliness (everything that deals with the spiritual man)".

<u>Just remember this, you are a healthy person. You are a prosperous individual. You are who God says you are.</u> If the situation looks different from what God has said, it is because Satan is trying to overflow us with his attack upon us. He's the deceiver and will try to make us think we are not who God says we are. **<u>BUT WE ARE WHO GOD SAYS WE ARE..</u>**

Chapter IV

WHEN THOU PASSEST THROUGH THE WATERS...

"But now thus saith the Lord that created thee, O Jacob, and he that formed thee, O Israel, Do not let your adversary intimidate you and cause you to be alarmed or frightened: for I have purchased you with a price, with the intent that I might set you free, I have called you by your name; and you belong to Me; you are Mine. When you pass through the waters, (notice it says "pass through" – it doesn't say "stay in") (the term "waters" there means a flooding type of water) when you pass through the floods, I will be with you; and through the rivers, they shall not overflow or inundate you or

Drag you under or cause you to be thoroughly washed away." Now, that's just pretty interesting right there; but let's go a step further. ". . .when thou walkest through the fire, thou shalt not be burned." When we are going through problems and situations, the Lord is always going to be there with us to take care of us. The original Hebrew word for "walk" means, "to depart; to cause to get away from; a way out." In other words, when we are on our way out of the fire, when we walk through, or depart from, or get away from the fire. . .we will not be burned. ". . .neither shall the flame kindle upon thee." The word "kindle" means to spark; to ignite; to cause to burn; to consume; to bring away or put away or take away or to waste. When we walk on our way out of the fire, we will not be burned; and the flame shall not kindle upon us. The word "flame" has both a masculine and a feminine gender. The masculine gender means a "flash" or "bright." The flash of the flame or the fire will not kindle upon us; will not ignite or consume or burn you. The feminine gender of "flame" means "the flaming head of a spear." So God is saying, "When thou walkest through – or in the process of your way out of the fire – it will not burn you or waste you away; and neither will the spark or the flash ignite upon your or cause you to be speared through by the fire with which the devil will come against you."

God has already said to us that we are not to allow the adversary to intimidate us or to cause us to be alarmed or frightened, because He has purchased us from the enemy in order that He might set us free. When we walk or pass through the floods, they will not drag us under or cause us to be washed away. And when we are in the midst of a fiery trial of our faith, that fire will not burn us nor will it consume us; neither will the spark ignite upon us. We will be delivered because He hath said, "I am the Lord thy God." Now, that's a good promise, isn't it?

The definition of flame which means, "the flaming head of a spear," brings to mind what Paul said in Ephesians 6:16 when he talked about putting on the whole armor of God. He said to take the shield of faith. . .(for what reason?), that we may be able to quench all of the fiery darts of the wicked. A dart is something that usually has a sharp point! Applying the feminine gender of "flame": ". . .neither shall the flame kindle upon you; neither shall the flaming head of a spear nor the polished blade nor the point of a weapon ignite or touch your life." Paul said it like this, "Above all, take the shield of faith, wherewith ye shall be a able to quench all the fiery darts of the wicked." (Ephesians 6:16)   Psalm 91 says something about this same thing. "He that dwelleth in the secret place of the most High shall abide under the shadow of the Almighty. I will say of the Lord, He is my refuge and my fortress: my God; in him will I trust. Surely he shall deliver thee from the snare of the fowler, and from the noisome pestilence. He shall cover thee with his feathers, and under his wings shalt thou trust: his truth shall be thy shield and buckler. Thou shalt not be afraid for the terror by night; **nor the arrow that flieth by day;"** The arrow that flieth by day is again a reference back to Isaiah 43; "neither shall the flaming head of a spear nor sword nor flaming head of an instrument of any kind come against you." He said we will not be afraid of the arrow that flies by day; "Nor for the pestilence that walketh in darkness,

A thousand shall fall at thy side, and ten thousand at thy right hand; but it shall not come nigh thee." It will not come near unto us.

In Isaiah He was again reaffirming that if we are in the place that God wants us to be; the fiery darts of the devil, that flaming fire with which he comes against us, will not even come near us. It will not kindle upon us. I will not ignite within us. It cannot even touch us because we have that armor of God upon us that protects us. Moses, when he was on the backside of the desert, saw a bush that was burning. He went over to see what it was and found that the bush was on fire but was not being burnt up. That's the same type of protection that God puts upon His children who will walk in Him and will dwell in His secret place and abide under the shadow of the Almighty. He said the flame shall not kindle against us and we will walk through the fire and not be burned. .The 3rd chapter of Daniel tells about three young men who had been taken captive into Babylon. They were Israelites, but their country had been captured and they were captives taken to Babylon. They found grace in the eyes of Nebuchadnezzar because God was working on their behalf. They were made princes and rulers in the land of Babylon. King Nebuchadnezzar decided that he would build a big idol that everybody would worship. He built a statue of pure gold, ninety feet tall and nine feet wide. Then he decided to have a dedication of this statue, so he called together all of those people who were in leadership in his country. When they were gathered together, he told them that when they heard the music play, everyone should bow down and worship the statue. That would dedicate the statue as a god in the country. The music played. The people bowed down. Some of the princes came to Nebuchadnezzar and told him that when the music played, the people bowed down, with the exception of three Hebrew young fellows named Shadrach, Meshach, and Abednego. They did not bow down. Nebuchadnezzar was quite upset about the situation and he called Shadrach, Meshach and Abednego to him and he said, "Gentlemen, what is this business? I commanded that all of you were to bow down when the music played, and I understand you didn't do it. I'm going to give you a second chance. Next time you hear the music, you bow down and you worship this god." "Shadrach, Meshach, and Abednego answered and said to the king, 'O Nebuchadnezzar, we are not careful to answer thee in this matter.' (We don't even have to think about it.) 'If it be so our God whom we serve is able to deliver us from the burning fiery furnace, and he will deliver us out of thine hand, O king. But if not, be it known unto thee, O king, that we will not serve thy gods, nor worship the golden image which thou hast set up.' Then was Nebuchadnezzar full of fury, and the form of his visage was changed against Shadrach, Meshach and Abednego;" (Daniel 3:16).

Look at what they said, most of us believe they answered, "O king, we don't have to think about it. He is our answer. If God wants to, He will deliver us out of the fiery furnace. If He doesn't want to, that's all right, we're going to serve Him anyway." That's not what they said. That's what we have thought they said, but that is not what they said. That's what we have thought they said, but that is not what they said. Nebuchadnezzar had said, "I'm going to give you a second chance." The three

Hebrew children said, "If you give us a second chance, bow down, because God is going to deliver us. If you don't give us a second chance, it doesn't make any difference. We're still not going to bow down." Those are the "ifs" they were talking about in that situation. There was never a question in their minds, whether or not God would deliver them. They never once said if God wants to He will, and if He doesn't want to, He won't. Their "if" was, "If you give us a second chance. . ." **They knew what God would do. You see, they had a covenant with Almighty God.** The covenant had been sealed with circumcision. They had shed blood and they had offered sacrifices. They had made a commitment with their God that everything they had was His and they would serve Him regardless of what happened God had said back to them, "Everything I have is yours and all you have to do is ask for it and it will be there."

Here is an interesting situation. Often, when people are away from home and where no-one knows them, they'll do things that they wouldn't do otherwise. You see, nobody would have known if they bowed down. Who would have said anything about it? They were thousands of miles away from home. All of their kinsfolk were gone. They were there by themselves. They could have bowed down and nobody would have thought a thing about it. They could have said, "Well, we're just doing what we have to to save our lives." But there comes a time when we have to take a stand for God, regardless of who is there or who is not there. We must make out stand for Jesus Christ, and no matter who says what or does what, we're going to stand firm for Him. Shadrach, Meshach and Abednego said, "King, we don't even have to think about it the second time. We don't even have to discuss it between ourselves. We have come to this conclusion. Our God is able to deliver us. If you give us a second chance, that's all right. We're still going to serve our God. If you don't give us a second chance, it doesn't make any difference. God will deliver us." Now that was faith! As a matter of fact, these three gentlemen are recorded in the 34th verse of the great chapter of faith, Hebrews 11; because they stood on the Word of God regardless of how circumstances looked.

    The king became so terribly angry that he called his other servants and he said, "I want you to pour more wood, more coal, more pitch, anything you can find into that furnace and I want you to heat it seven times hotter than it's ever been heated in its." Now that's how mad he got. It is similar to the madness that was upon the people as they were stoning Stephen to death. They got so mad that they literally bit him. They gnashed upon him with their teeth, the Bible says. Can you imagine grown men getting so mad that they start biting? Can you imagine an individual in the position of king of a nation becoming so engrossed in his fury that he heated the furnace seven times hotter than it had ever been heated before and saying, "I am going to show you." Daniel 3 records that, it was so hot in that furnace, and the force of that intense heat was so great, that when they opened the door the flame just leaped out; and the men who threw Shadrach, Meshach, and Abednego in were consumed instantly by the blast of heat.

The furnace began to burn down just a little bit. The king went over to see what had happened. Now why would he go to see see what had happened? His men had already been killed, yet he went over to see what was going on. Then the king rose up and said to one of his counselors, "Didn't we throw three men in there? Something strange is going on." He went to the window of the furnace and peeked in and saw Shadrach, Meshach and Abednego. . . and another man in there walking around with them. The Word says they were walking around in the midst of the fire. **"When thou walkest through the fire, thou shalt not be burned."** They were walking around in there and the king said, "That fourth man looks like the Son of God." Well, friend, He not only looked like a God; but He was God. For did not He say, "When thou walkest through the fire, thou shalt not be burned; neither shall the flame kindle upon thee, for I am the Lord thy God." And just before that He said, **"I will be with you."** God was in there with them, and He put around them His asbestos covering that caused Shadrach, Meshach and Abednego to walk around in the midst of the fire and not even be burned. So they opened the door of the furnace and they let Shadrach, Meshach and Abednego out. Further comments were made concerning the strangeness of this situation. In verse 26 it says, "Then Nebuchadnezzar came near to the mouth of the burning fiery furnace, and spake, and said, 'Shadrach, Meshach, and Abednego, ye servants of the most high God, come forth, and come hither.' Then Shadrach, Meshach, and Abednego came forth of the midst of the fire. And the princes, governors, and captains, and the king's counselors, being gathered together, saw these men, upon whose bodies the fire had no power, nor was an hair of their head singed..."

A few years ago, the furnace in our

church had gone out, and I went over to re-light it. I couldn't get it going but I turned the gas on, and finally, I stuck a match and suddenly there was an explosion that knocked me back about four or five feet against the wall. I looked around, and the hair on the back of my hands and across my head and my eyes, my eyebrows, everything, had been singed from the flame that came out. I know what it's like to have hair singed. But Daniel says that the hair of their heads was not even singed; and the furnace was seven times hotter than it had ever been in all of its existence. "neither were their coats changed. . ." It didn't even scorch their clothes. "nor the smell of fire had passed on them." They didn't even smell like they had been close to smoke. There was no smell of smoke on them. "Fear not, for I am with thee. I have redeemed thee. I have called thee by thy name. Thou art mine. When thou passest through the waters, I will be with thee. Through the rivers, they shall not overflow thee. When thou walkest through the fire, thou shalt not be burned; neither shall the flame kindle upon you. For I am the Lord thy God, the Holy One, they Savior."

I don't suppose any of us will be exempt from fiery trials and tests. As a matter of fact, this prophecy in Isaiah 43 did not say that we would not go through fire. It did not way that we would not go through the flood. But it said that in the midst of the flood, and in the midst of the fire, God would be with us. There are many times when we ask God to totally take us out of situations that were He to do so, God would completely negate His plan and purpose for our lives. But He said, "When you walk through the valley of the shadow of death, I will be with you." His rod and His staff shall comfort us. "When thou walkest through the fire, thou shalt not be burned; neither will the flame kindle upon you. When thou passest through the flood, it will not overflow you. And through the rivers, they will not drag you under."

All who live godly lives in Christ Jesus will suffer persecutions, but the Lord knows how to deliver us out of them all. "There is no temptation taken you but such as is common unto man; but with that temptation He will make a way of escape" (I Corinthians 10:13). No matter how difficult or even hopeless any situation appears to be, even if it seems we have been covered over by the waters that Satan is trying to flood against us; the Word of God says that the Spirit of the Lord will lift up a standard when the enemy comes in like a flood. The Lord has said to put on the whole armor of God, that we might be able to withstand. Fear not, because God is with us. If we are putting our trust in God and in the Lord Jesus Christ, there is nothing that will take us; there is nothing that will hurt us; there is nothing that can destroy us; there is nothing that can drag us under. God has something for us and He will provide for us when it seems like the devil has closed every other door. There is a way out. God has a fire escape. Glory to God! And we will go through it and not even our hair will be singed nor will the smell of smoke be upon us. God is working in our lives no matter what we are going through. It may even seem to us that we have suffering wrong and the person who did the wrong is prospering and doing well. But God is not going to leave us in that fire. God is not going to leave us with that flood, flooding over us. He overcame, and we will overcome also because **"greater is He that is in us than he**

that is in the world." We can walk through the fire and we will not be burned.

GLORY TO GOD!

In every situation God is right by our side to meet our need. Of course, we must know Jesus Christ as our personal Savior in order to claim and receive all these benefits. God is merciful, and He has our guardian angel working in our behalf to protect us so that we can be drawn to Him. But to claim the benefits of these promises of God, we must be abiding in the Lord. Psalm 91 tells about the arrow that flies by day and that it shall not come near us. That is only if we are **abiding under the shadow of the Almighty and dwelling in the secret place of the Most High**. All of these promises are contingent on knowing Jesus as our personal Savior. But if we know Jesus Christ as our Lord and Savior, we need not let anything or anyone discourage us, or cause us to consider giving up; because God is going to be with us. He will not leave us nor forsake us. He will go with us even to the end of the earth. There is no place we can go that Jesus is not there. There is nothing we can do that Jesus is not there. Jesus is always there. David said, "I can go down to the pit and He is there. Anywhere on this earth I go, God is there." You see, it doesn't make any difference what we're doing, God is there doing it with us. He loves us that much.

The thing that excited me as much as anything else one time was to learn that while I was sitting in geometry class, which I hated; God was sitting right there hating it with me. But He was there because I was there. He loved me that much. I don't think He liked it a bit better than I did, but He was there with me because He loved me.

God loves us enough that He is here with us and He will not allow us to be tempted above that which we are able to bear; He will make a way of escape for us. Whether our need is a business need, a family situation, a personal need, or any other need – God will never allow us, if we put our trust in Him, to be tempted above that which we are able to bear. **"The flame will not kindle upon you and neither shall you be burned."**

5

Chapter V

I AM THE LORD YOUR GOD

"Now thus saith the Lord that created thee, O Jacob, and formed thee O Israel; do not let your adversary intimidate you or cause you to be alarmed or frightened; because I have purchased you with My blood. I have redeemed you, that you might be set free. I have called you by your name. I know who you are; and you are Mind. When you pass through the floods, I will be with you; and through the rivers, they shall not inundate you or drag you under or thoroughly wash you away. When you make your way through the fire, you will not be burned; neither shall the spark, or the shining blade of the enemy, kindle upon you For I am the Lord thy God, the Holy One of Israel, they Savior. I gave Egypt for your ransom, and Ethiopia and Seba for thee."

As we read again the first three verses of Isaiah 43, seeing the various things that we may go through in life, realizing that we all face struggles at some time or other in our lives, realizing that there are times that seem as though we are about to be pulled down and dragged under, walking through fire and everything else, we hear the Lord say, **"Don't be afraid."** We hear Him speak and say, "I'll be with you; and there's no reason for you to be fearful or alarmed."

Now, there are a lot of people who could tell us not to be alarmed or afraid, because they're going to be with us; and it wouldn't mean anything at all. Why is it that we should feel encouraged or strengthened or unafraid, when God says, "I'll be with you; don't be afraid?" There has to be something to back up God's statement that would cause us not to be afraid or alarmed. There has to be some power or ability in Him that we could recognize, that would cause us to be able to say, "If God says don't be afraid, I won't be afraid; or if He says that He will be with me through the floods and through the fire, and it will not burn me nor will the smell of smoke be upon me; then I will not be afraid, because He is there".

A fellow was telling a minister about the problems he was facing in life; and as he faced one problem right after the other, he was confused and alarmed and needed help. He talked to the pastor on several occasions and finally the pastor asked him, "What really is it that you need"? The man looked the minister straight in the eye and said,

"I need a new God". Now you say, "We don't need a new God. There is only one God". What the man was saying is more true than most of us realize. **But many of us do need a new understanding of Who God is**. We have made everything else their god, and even our idea of the true God is wrong; we think of Him as some austere being out there somewhere, ready to slap us at the least little moment of disobedience or failure. The man said, "I need a new God"; and what he was saying was really the truth. The reason so many of us struggle is because we do need a new concept or revelation of what God is really all about.

Not all of our struggles are internal. Some of our struggles are with society and outward situations; and sometimes we progress rather slowly in some areas of our lives. Every one of us has his share of those things which seem impossible to surmount

surmount and various problems and struggles that we face every day; and we need this **new** revelation of God for our **old** struggles. As I read this particular passage of scripture, "For I am the Lord thy God, the Holy One of Israel", I was reminded of the story of a man by the name of Moses, who was out on the back side of the desert in Midian, minding his father-in-law's sheep. Moses was there because forty years before that, he had fled from Egypt. There he, a Jewish boy, had been reared in the home of the Egyptian Pharaoh, as the son of the daughter of the Pharaoh; with all of the prestige of belonging there. Yet, in his spirit, he knew that something was not as it ought to be. As he was growing up, his mother had taught him that he was not really an Egyptian, but that he was a Jewish boy; and that some day he would be instrumental in bringing the people of Israel out of their

Moses tried to get ahead of God; you know the story; and he had to flee for his life. As Moses was tending the sheep, he saw a bush that was burning, but not being consumed; and he heard a voice say to him, "Moses, Moses"; and he answered, "Lord, here am I. What do You want?" God said, "I'm going to deliver the people of Israel. I've heard their prayer and their cry." Moses reacted as most of us probably would have; he said, "If You're with me and with my people, then how come they're in bondage and slavery down there? If you're really with us, how come we're going through all of this junk?" Have you ever asked God that question? Have you ever questioned the Lord like Habakkuk did when he said, "Lord, why is it that these nations that are worse than we are doing better than we are?" Have you ever questioned and said, "Why is it that this man who is a terrible, wicked, vile, sinner is doing better than I am?" Have you ever asked that question? Habakkuk asked it. Moses asked it. There were others who asked the same question. Moses asked, "Where are You now, Lord? Don't you know what's happening to Your people down there? Don't You understand, Lord? Don't you care? Does it not matter to you? Can't You do something about it?" He was questioning the Lord, and God said, "Yes, I understand. I care; and I'm going to do something about it."

When Moses was ready, and when the right time had come, Moses had this encounter with God that changed his way and changes his life. God told Moses that He knew of the suffering of the people of Israel, and He knew that He would be there to deliver them out of the bondage that they were in in Egypt. Moses, perhaps a little frightened, stood before God and said,

"Lord, if I go down there and tell them that You're going to deliver us, why would they listen to me? Who am I to tell them has sent me? I tried once before. Why would they listen to me now?" The answer that Moses received introduced him to a new God, as far as Moses was concerned. He was introduced to a new Supreme Being who was able to take care of the struggles of His people; and He simply said, **"I AM THAT I AM"** Moses said, "What do you mean, I Am who I Am?" God said, "Tell those people I Am hath sent you." In the book of Exodus, the third chapter and the fourteenth verse, God's exact words were, **"I AM THAT I AM:"** and "Thus shalt thou say unto the Children of Israel, **I AM** hath sent me unto you."

The word **"I AM"** that God used here was the first time that this word had ever been used; it was a new name that had never

Been given before, concerning God, which signified the nature and the character of God. God said, "I AM hath sent you." This same word is used in Isaiah 43, verse 3, "For I am the Lord they God;" this told of the nature of God; it had a special meaning and significance; and it's based on the Hebrew infinitive which is **"hayah"**, or "to be; or to cause to happen." When **"Yah"** is added to **"hayah"**, then it says, "I AM the God who will make things happen. I AM the One who is going to cause things to come into existence and to happen." God said, "Go tell them that I AM hath sent you. Go down there and tell them 'I AM the One who causes things to happen' has sent you." You see, God is the Lord of creation. In Isaiah 43:3, God says, "I am the Lord;" so we have two words here, "Yahweh" and "Jehovah;" "I AM the One Who creates things and causes them to happen," and the word

Jehovah", which means, "the God Who is self-existent; or the person Who is the self-existent One;" in other words, "I AM not a created One; I AM the One Who creates, and I cause things to happen: I AM the Lord; I AM the self-existent One Who causes things to happen and creates things for the needs of My people." That's what He said when He said, "I AM THE LORD THY GOD."

God is the Lord of creation. God is the Lord of our destiny; He is the Lord of our circumstances; He is the Lord of our victories; He is the Lord, Who brings us victoriously through our struggles. This is exactly what Moses and God's people needed to know. They needed to know "I AM" would help them. They needed to know that there was someone who really would meet their need; that He would act on their behalf; that He would do what was necessary to liberate and bring deliverance into their lives. Here's what the Lord was saying in Exodus, the sixth chapter, verses two, three and six: "And God spoke unto Moses, and said unto him, I am the Lord." The word for "God is the plural, "Elohim." "Elohim" said, "I am the Lord: And I appeared unto Abraham, unto Isaac, and unto Jacob, by the name of God Almighty", which is 'El Shaddai', the all-sufficient One. The word "Lord", in verse 2, was "Yahweh". "I am the Lord; I appeared unto Abraham, Isaac and Jacob as 'God Almighty', 'El Shaddai'. Let's look at it this way; "Elohim said to Moses, 'Yahweh' appeared unto Abraham, Isaac and Jacob as 'El Shaddai'. What does this mean? "The Almighty God said to Moses; the One who creates things and causes things to happen, appeared unto Abraham, Isaac and Jacob as the One Who is the all-sufficient One."

Let's read on in Exodus 6:3, **"but by my name Jehovah was I not known to them; Wherefore say unto the Children of Israel, I am the Lord, and I will bring you out from under the burdens of the Egyptians, and I will rid you out of their bondage..."**.

God was not only El Shaddai, the Provider; but now He was the Creator, the One who caused things to happen; the One who would bring deliverance; the One who would cause them to go through the floods and through the fires, and yet not be covered nor be burned. He said, **"I am the Lord thy God."** Do you know that same Lord is alive today and works today? We were never meant to struggle alone. The promise made to Moses is the same promise that's made to us; "I'll be with you. I'll make things happen for you." I want some of you to pay attention to that very closely, because you have you've been wondering if God could make anything miraculous happen for you. Let me just say this to you: **The same promise that God made to Moses when He said, "I'll make things happen for you," He makes to you today;** "I will cause things to happen for you." Do you see what this is saying? God said, "I AM". Now, the word "I AM" means the One who creates things and causes them to come into existence. "I AM" has said to you, "Don't be afraid." God says to you, "I will create whatever is necessary to meet your need. If it's not available, I'll make it. I am the Creator; and I will cause things to come into existence for you, to take care of your struggles in your life. When you go through the floods, "I AM" with you."

Here's something that's very interesting. In the third century, after and birth and death of Christ, these passages were being translated into Greek from Hebrew, so that the Jews who were scattered all around the world (some of whom were living in Greece) could read the scripture in the Greek language. The verb "to be" or "to make happen" was translated in the present tense. In the Greek, the divine name "Yahweh" is "Ego eimi"; in the present tense, "Ego eimi" says, "I am the One who makes things happen now." God said to Moses, and He said in Isaiah, "Yahweh", "I will make things happen." Now instead of saying, "I am the God who 'will' make things happen" He says, "I am the God who makes things happen right now. I am your Lord; the self-existent One; the Holy One of Israel, your Savior. I AM the One who makes things happen now."

We can trust in Him to forgive the past. We can trust in Him and surrender the future to Him, because all of the "now" aspect of God is here. God said, "I will take care of the past, and I will take care of the future. I am the present One that causes things to happen right now in your life".

Knowing that God can make things happen doesn't do us one bit of good, if we don't know the One who can make things happen. It's one thing to know about Him, and to know what He can do; it's another thing to know Him personally. That's why "Yahweh" had to come into history and live among us. The gospel of John begins by saying "In the beginning was the Word, and the Word was with God, and the Word was God." Further in that same passage it says, "And the Word was made flesh, and dwelt among us, (and we beheld his glory, the glory as of the only begotten of the Father,) full of grace and truth"; then it reads, "For the law was given by Moses, but grace and truth came by Jesus Christ. No man hath seen God at any time; the only begotten Son, which is in the bosom of the Father, He hath declared him". Do you know what that means to us? That means that this "Jesus", who lived on earth about 2,000 years ago, who wrought miracles, and preached concerning the Kingdom of Heaven, who died on a cross, was put in a tomb, and rose again on the third day; that means this same "Jesus" is the very "Yahweh" of the Old Testament. Jesus is the very God that made things happen then; and is still making things happen; and will continue to make things happen.

Jesus Christ is "God with us", in all of the struggles of our life. When we go through the floods; when we walk through the fire, God is with us. It wouldn't have done one bit of good for Isaiah to have said, "Don't be afraid, when you go through the floods; and don't be alarmed when you pass

pass through the fire. . .", if this next statement had never come; the statement that said, "For I am the Lord thy God, the Holy One, thy Savior". If that had not been there, all of the other wouldn't have meant a thing. It doesn't mean any thing for me to tell you, "Don't be afraid, when you're going through the storms of your life", unless I have the power to back up what I'm saying. Almighty God has the power to back up anything that He says; and when He tells you, "I will go with you through the flood", He will go with you through the flood. When He tells you not to fear when you walk through the valley of the shadow of death, there is no reason for you to be afraid; because He will be there with you. When God tells you that when you walk through the fire, you will not be burned because He will be walking through that fire with you; you can rest assured that He will do it! God is not a man that He should lie; but He will do that which He has said that He will do.

This is something that every one of us needs to know. In the words of Jesus Christ, twenty-two times in the Gospel of John, we hear Jesus assume His Divine authority when He says, in relationship to sin, sickness, sadness, disease, and all afflictions, "I AM"; "Ego eimi"; I AM the One who creates things and causes them to happen right now". That's all we need to know in our struggles. We don't need to know anything else! **All we need to know is Jesus.**

Reverend R. W. Schambach says, "You don't have any trouble; all you need is faith in God." You don't need to know anything else, other than that Jesus Christ is the Living God, Himself; and He walks with us in the midst of our struggles; He walks with us every day of our lives. Everywhere

Everywhere that we go, He is there with us, constantly abiding in our hearts and lives. That's all we need to know, because He is there to give us advice; He is there to admonish us; He is there to give us all of the things that we need.

What most of us need to know, is that the God who lived among us as the Lord Jesus Christ, the **"I AM"** who revealed His life and His blessings unto us, intends to live within our lives, as well. In the Gospel of John, Jesus told the people, **"If ye continue in my word, then are ye my disciples indeed; And ye shall know the truth, and the truth shall make you free"**. These words brought a very angry response from the Jews; they were upset over this. They said, "We are descendants of Abraham; and we've never been in bondage to anyone. How is it that You say, 'ye shall know the truth, and the truth shall make ye free."

How is it that You can say that we shall be made free"? Jesus simply said, "Verily, verily, I say unto you, Before Abraham was, I Am". Listen to that, "Before Abraham ever was, I Am. I was existing before He was. I am existing now. I will exist long after you're dead and gone. Before Abraham ever was, I Am". Jesus was claiming to be the very author of Abraham's faith; He was claiming to be the very beginning of everything; He said, "I am; always have been; always will be". It was undeniable claim that Jesus made. He was saying, "I am the pre-existent Christ. I am the One who was before all things." This assertion that Jesus made about Himself kept the Jews at a point of not understanding, and almost speechless. You see, if we accept God as the ultimate "I AM", the uncreated Creator, then all of the rest of His "I AM's" will flash and sparkle like diamonds under a brilliant light. We listen to Jesus as He says, "I AM; have no fear! I AM the light of the world. I AM the bread of life. I AM the good shepherd", and our hearts leap within us. We listen to Him as He says, "I AM come that you might have life, and have it more abundantly. I AM the way, the truth and the life. No man comes to the Father, but by Me. I AM the resurrection and the life. Anyone who believes in Me shall never die, but shall live for eternity. I AM the true vine. I AM with you always, even unto the end of the earth. I AM the Lord thy God, the Holy One of Israel, they Savior".

Do you believe that Jesus is who He says He is? Is He truly God? Is He truly God with you, and therefore the Lord over all of your life and your circumstances? Is He able to marshal all power in Heaven and earth to meet your needs? Do you believe that? Do you really believe that Jesus performed miracles in the physical, emotional and spiritual struggles of the lives of the people when He was here? Do you dare to believe that He can and will perform these same miracles today in your life? Can He who is the Creator, the Sustainer, the Innovator of all that happens in this world make things happen in your life? Are you willing to ask Him to be the triumphant "I AM" in the specific struggles of your life? Most of us readily agree that we believe Jesus is who He says He is, and that He has power to marshal the forces of Heaven to meet the needs of people. Most of us believe that Jesus performed miracles when He was here on this earth, every kind of miracle regarding the needs of people. The question that some of us hesitate at, though, is, **"Do you believe that Jesus will meet those same needs in your life, with His same miraculous power"?** You may think

"Oh, I know He can do it for someone else; but for me, that's something else. I'm not too sure about that".

Let me tell you something. If you're willing to ask Jesus to be the triumphant "I AM" of your life, there's not a struggle you'll go through but that I AM Yahweh, Jehovah, El Shaddai, Jehovah-nissi" will be there to meet the need of your life. **That self-existent One who causes things to happen, and creates things right now, is here to meet the need of your life;** and He says, "Thus saith the Lord, the self-existent One who created you; the "I AM"; the one who formed you; don't be intimidated by the adversary, or be alarmed or frightened; because I, Jehovah, Yahweh, the Creator of all the universe, have redeemed you; I have bought back you and everything that was sold by Adam to Satan; I have bought it all back with the purpose of setting you free.

I have called you by your name, and you belong to Me. When you pass through the floods, I will be with you. When you go through the rivers, they shall not drag you under, nor thoroughly wash you away. When you make your way out of the fire, you shall not be burned; neither shall that spark ignite and kindle and burn and consume upon you; for I am the Creator, the One who has made you and formed you, and the One who causes things to happen now, the Lord thy God, the Holy One of Israel; and I am your Savior."

Do you know God as your Lord and your Savior? Have you made Him that triumphant One? Is He the real Controller of your heart and of your life? If He is not, I urge you right now to make Jesus the Lord of your life; because He is the One who can create things and cause them to happen now. God still creates today. I have read testimonies of people who have had certain organs of their bodies surgically removed, and later after prayer, doctors would examine them and find there were brand new organs inside their bodies. We have also experienced this in our own ministry, new arteries, new spleen, new blood, removing hepatitis from the person completely. **<u>God is still in the creating business, friend. There has been no change in God.</u>** This is what I like about God; He can create all the angels He wants, but Satan cannot create one more demon than what he had to start with. God can continue to make and create other worlds if He desires to, and He may be doing that very thing.

God said, "**<u>I AM, I AM, I AM</u>** the God who creates things and causes things to happen; and **I AM YOUR GOD**. I have called you by your name. You belong to me.

Me." He is my God. He is my personal deliverer.

You need to declare today that Jesus Christ is the Lord of your life. He is your redeemer, and you are His.

2 Timothy 1:7 **"*For God has not given us a spirit of fear; but of power, and of love, and of a sound mind.*"**

I WILL NOT FEAR FOR GOD IS WITH ME.

A SINNER'S PRAYER
TO RECEIVE JESUS AS SAVIOR

Dear Heavenly Father ...

I come to you in the name of Jesus. You said in your word, "Whosoever shall call upon the name of the Lord shall be saved" (Romans 10:13). I am calling upon Your name, so I know You are saving me now.

You also said, "That if thou shalt confess with thy mouth the Lord Jesus, and shall believe in thy heart that God has raised him from the dead, thou shall be saved. For with the heart man believes unto righteousness; and with the mouth confession is made unto salvation" (Romans 10:9-10). I believe in my heart Jesus Christ is the Son of God. I believe that He was raised from the dead for my justification. And I confess Him now as by Lord, because your word says, "With the heart man believes unto righteousness" and I do believe with my heart.

I have now become the righteousness of God in Christ (2 Corinthians 5:21). I am Saved!
Thank you Lord.

If you said this prayer and accepted Jesus as you savior please let us know.

Name_____

Address_____

City_____

State_____**Zip**_____

OTHER BOOKS BY ARMAN STEPHENS

ANGELS WON'T AND DEVILS CAN'T
HOW TO SLAY A GIANT
THE DAY DEATH DIED
BORN TO PRAISE

BY DEE STEPHENS

NUGGETS
NAMES OF GOD GREETING CARDS

TO ORDER WRITE TO

FTLB PUBLICATIONS
P.O. BOX 970
BETHANY, OK. 73008

OR E-MAIL
Pastorarman@msn.com

TAPE SERIES

PSALMS 91

REAP YOUR HARVEST

I WOULD HAVE FAINTED

THE POWER OF SPEAKING IN TONGUES

GO TO THE OTHER SIDE

LORD TEACH US TO PRAY

THE KINGDOM IS LIKE…..

TO ORDER WRITE TO

FTLB PUBLICATIONS
P.O. BOX 970
BETHANY, OK. 73008

OR E-MAIL
Pastorarman@msn.com